The Battle of Kadesh: The History of the Most Important Battle Between the Egyptians and Hittites

By Charles River Editors

A relief inside Ramesses II's Abu Simbel temple that depicts him firing arrows from a chariot during the Battle of Kadesh

Introduction

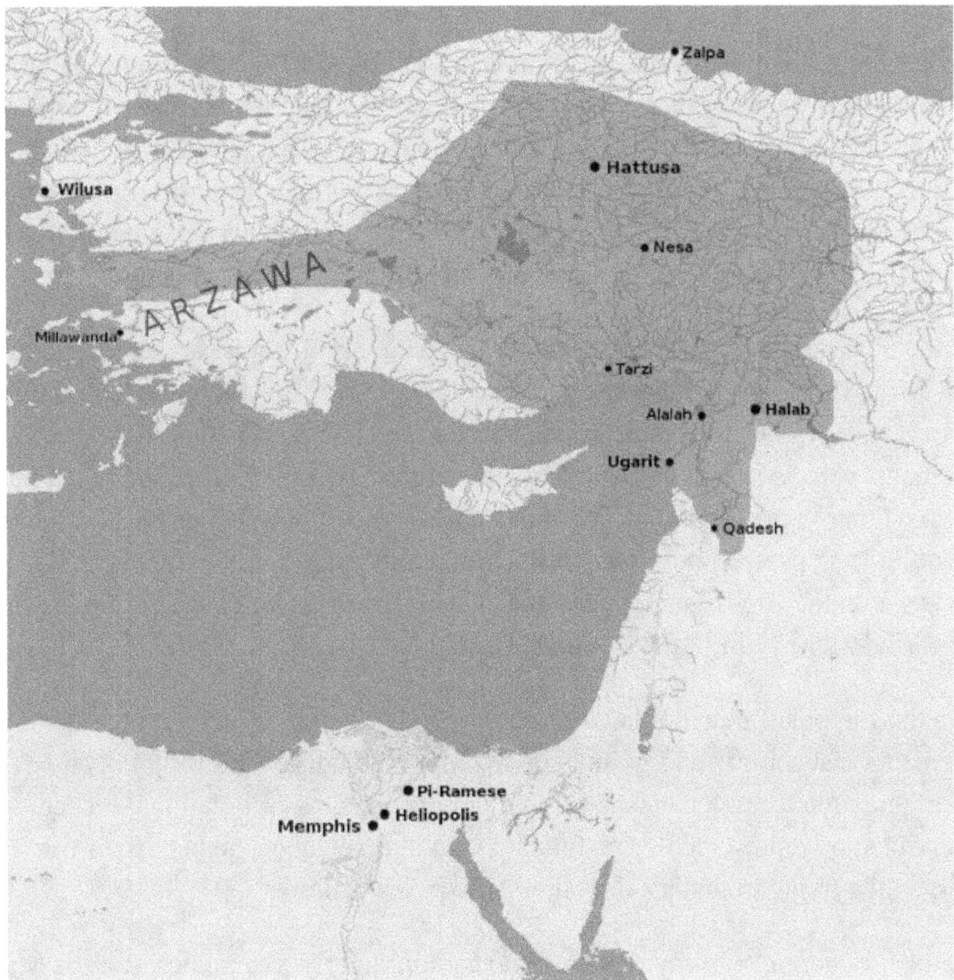

The Egyptian Empire (green) and the Hittite Empire (red) circa 1279 BCE

"Now then, his majesty had prepared his infantry, his chariotry, and the Sherden of his majesty's capturing...in the Year 5, 2nd month of the third season, day 9, his majesty passed the fortress of Sile. [and entered Canaan] ... His infantry went on the narrow passes as if on the highways of Egypt. Now after days had passed after this, then his majesty was in Ramses Meri-Amon, the town which is in the Valley of the Cedar." – An Egyptian inscription detailing the campaign

Africa may have given rise to the first human beings, and Egypt probably gave rise to the first great civilizations, which continue to fascinate modern societies across the globe nearly 5,000 years later. From the Library and Lighthouse of Alexandria to the Great Pyramid at Giza, the ancient Egyptians produced several wonders of the world, revolutionized architecture and construction, created some of the world's first systems of mathematics and medicine, and established language and art that spread across the known world. With famous leaders like King Tut and Cleopatra, it's no wonder that today's world has so many Egyptologists.

What makes the accomplishments of the ancient Egyptians all the more remarkable is that Egypt was historically a place of great political turbulence. Its position made it both valuable and vulnerable to tribes across the Mediterranean and the Middle East, and Egypt had no shortage of its own internecine warfare. Its most famous conquerors would come from Europe, with Alexander the Great laying the groundwork for the Hellenic Ptolemy line and the Romans extinguishing that line after defeating Cleopatra and driving her to suicide.

Perhaps the most intriguing aspect of ancient Egyptian civilization was its inception from the ground up, as the Egyptians themselves had no prior civilization which they could use as a template. In fact, Egypt itself became a template for the civilizations that followed. The Greeks and the Romans were so impressed with Egyptian culture that they often attributed many aspects of their own culture to the Egyptians. With that said, some minor elements of ancient Egyptian culture were, indeed, passed on to later civilizations. Egyptian statuary appears to have had an initial influence on the Greek version, and the ancient Egyptian language continued long after the pharaonic period in the form of the Coptic language.

Although the Egyptians may not have passed their civilization directly on to later civilizations, the key elements that comprised Egyptian civilization, including their religion, early ideas of state, and art and architecture, can be seen in other pre-modern civilizations. Indeed, since Egyptian civilization represented some fundamental human concepts, historians often turn to their history when trying to understand other pre-modern cultures.

Many battles fought in antiquity remain famous thousands of years later, such as Marathon, Thermopylae, and Cannae, mainly due to the belligerents involved and the ways in which the battles changed the course of history. However, even as people are fascinated by the Egyptians, one of the most important battles in antiquity has also been one of the most overlooked: the Battle of Kadesh, fought by Ramesses II against the Hittites.

Seeking to spread the area of Egypt's influence and control, Ramesses II led his first military campaign as pharaoh into Canaan in 1275 BCE.[1] There were many battles fought during this campaign, but the one that is recorded in most detail describes Ramesses II fighting one of the Canaanite princes. This prince was apparently wounded by an arrow before his army was broken and routed by the Egyptian force. In the aftermath of the battle, the other princes of Canaan were made prisoners by Ramesses II, captured, and sent back to Egypt as their lands were plundered by the pharaoh's troops. Cowed by Egypt's military power, these vassal lands were thereafter forced to provide tribute to Egypt every year, which Ramesses II received himself at ruling headquarters he set up for himself in Riblah.[2]

---

[1] Grimal, Nicolas. 1994. *A History of Ancient Egypt*. Wiley, USA. pp 253.

The Hittite vassal state of Amurru was another one of those captured on this military campaign, and the expansion of Egypt's forces into their territory was of great concern to the rulers of the Hittite Empire. Hittite forces posed a threat to Ramesses II and his ambitions, but his early military successes only led him to plan even further expansion for his empire. It was this expansionist attitude that would lead directly to the Battle of Kadesh in the fifth year of his reign.

In order to achieve his dreams of conquest, Ramesses II needed a constant supply of trained forces and a vast cache of weapons. With his ambitions now clearly defined, the Pharaoh set about creating an industry of war after setting up a new capital he dubbed Pi-Ramesses. This military industry was primarily set up to support another planned campaign into Hittite territory; the capital of Pi-Ramesses was located to the northeast of Cairo in the region of the Nile delta, inland from Tanis and the Mediterranean Sea, and the position of the city itself was possibly motivated by military reasoning.

At Pi-Ramesses, the pharaoh had factories set up with one very clear objective: the swift and successful manufacture of the tools of war. The weapons that were crafted there included spears, swords, shields, and chariots. The official records state that these were turned out at a rate of 1,000 weapons per week and 1,000 shields every week and a half. The larger and more complex construction required for chariot building meant that only around 250 were completed every fortnight.[3]

With the energy and industry of Egypt turned to this purpose, it was not long before Ramesses II had the tools he required to make his ambitions a reality. He wanted nothing less than to destroy the Hittite Empire and claim their territory for his own, and it was toward that end that he led his troops into the Levant in 1274 BCE.[4]

The main battle of the campaign took place outside the moderately important city of Kadesh, which was located in modern Syria. Although Egyptologists, historians, and archaeologists of the ancient Near East are quite familiar with the battle, outside of a few references in films that concern Exodus, it has failed to capture the popular imagination, despite its critical importance.

For one thing, it is the earliest known pitched battle to be documented, and the number of troops deployed by both the Egyptians and Hittites may have made it the largest battle ever fought up until that point in time. The organization of the forces, especially the Egyptians, is another intriguing aspect of this battle, because the Egyptians organized their units into divisions, which may be the first such case in history or simply the first time the organization was recorded.

Arguably the most famous aspect of the battle is that it was passed down in ways that barely

---

[2] Grimal, Nicolas. 1994. *A History of Ancient Egypt*. Wiley, USA. pp 253.
[3] Tyldesley, Joyce. 2001. *Ramesses: Egypt's Greatest Pharaoh*. Penguin. pp 68.
[4] Tyldesley, Joyce. 2001. *Ramesses: Egypt's Greatest Pharaoh*. Penguin. pp 68.

aligned with reality. Surrounded and swiftly outnumbered, most of the Egyptian soldiers were killed in the battle, and Ramesses II was forced to retreat in order to survive. What is known of the rest of the battle is that the pharaoh rallied his forces, fought on through the battlefield in order to evade capture and death, and managed to get away with only with a fraction of his troops, while the majority of his army lay slain on the field of battle that he left behind him.[5]

Nonetheless, the battle essentially ended in a stalemate, after which there was a period of extended peace and eventually an alliance between the Egyptians and Hittites. The ensuing peace also helped to solidify the Late Bronze Age Near Eastern geopolitical system modern scholars often refer to as the "Great Powers Club," during which the most powerful empires of the Near East tended to use diplomacy instead of warfare to settle their differences.

Of course, that wasn't good enough for Ramesses II, who turned the tactical setback into a propaganda victory the world had never seen before. The hopes Ramesses II had held for claiming for Egypt both the city and territory around Kadesh were lost, but Ramesses II had survived, and when he returned to Egypt, he set out to test the adage that history is written by the winners. Ramesses II erected monuments, commissioned inscriptions, and oversaw the decoration of reliefs all proclaiming the Battle of Kadesh as a major victory. His personal heroism and skill as a warrior were praised on inscriptions at such locations as Abydos, the Ramesseum, Karnak, Luxor, and Abu Simbel. Ramesses had personal details inscribed that claimed, "No officer was with me, no charioteer, no soldier of the army, no shield-bearer..." and "I was before them like Seth in his monument. I found the mass of chariots in whose midst I was, scattering them before my horses..." In Luxor, it was written, "His majesty slaughtered the armed forces of the Hittites in their entirety, their great rulers and all their brothers ... their infantry and chariot troops fell prostrate, one on top of the other. His majesty killed them ... and they lay stretched out in front of their horses. But his majesty was alone, nobody accompanied him..."[6] If the inscriptions were to be believed, the pharaoh had singlehandedly ensured his own survival, even with all the odds stacked against him.

Ramesses II successfully used propaganda inscribed onto the monuments and in the public places of Egypt to ensure that the people he ruled would deem him a victorious leader, even when he himself was faced with defeat. Even before the Battle of Kadesh, Ramesses II was certainly no stranger to the concept of propaganda, as his father had used such techniques to legitimize his family bloodline, glorifying his own military prowess and ensuring the succession of his son. Ramesses II was fully aware that a pharaoh's legacy was written in stone, ensuring the survival of his name through the deeds that he himself chose to record. To say it worked would be an understatement, as Ramesses the Great remains one of the most famous Egyptians of all.

---

[5] Kuhrt, Amélie. 1995. *The Ancient Near East, C. 3000-330 BCE*. Routledge, USA. pp 258.
[6] Lichtheim, Miriam. 1976. *Ancient Egyptian Literature: The New Kingdom*. University of California Press, Berkeley. pp 62.

The Battle of Kadesh: The History of the Most Important Battle Between the Egyptians and Hittites

Ancient History's Most Documented Battle

Perhaps the most unique element of the Battle of Kadesh is how well it was documented in the Egyptian annals. The Egyptians had a well-developed historiographical tradition by the time the battle took place sometime around 1285 BCE, including king-lists, annals, and biographical inscriptions that began in the Old Kingdom and continued through the Late Period (Redford 1986). It must be pointed out, though, that the Egyptian concept of historical writing had a different function or purpose than historical writing today. The Egyptians recorded important events but did not comment on how or why those events happened, other than possibly assigning a divine agent, nor did they ponder the implications of those events. Still, Egyptian historiography was an impressive tradition, and the records of the Battle of Kadesh are the apogee of that tradition in many ways. After all, the fact that Kadesh is considered the best documented battle prior to the Battle of Marathon in 490 BCE is certainly historically important in itself (Redford 1992, 184).

Egyptian scribes produced six different versions of the battle that were inscribed on the walls of temples throughout Egypt. The version at the Abydos Temple was probably the oldest, but it is also the most fragmentary and therefore the least helpful in terms of details. The Karnak Temple has two versions, the Ramesseum has two, and three versions can be found at the Luxor Temple. The Abu Simbel Temple in Nubia also has a condensed version (Spalinger 2005, 209). Most versions were accompanied by pictorial reliefs, which have further aided historians in determining the types of weapons, armor, and chariots both sides used. The pictorial reliefs have also been useful for identifying some of the battlefield details, including which troops did the majority of the fighting and how they moved during the battle. The written versions are also commonly divided into two forms or genres: a more flowery poem and a standard military bulletin (Shaw and Nicholson 1995, 236). There is also a cuneiform letter Ramesses II wrote to Huttusili III (r. c. 1275-1245 BCE), the successor of Muwatalli II (r. c. 1295-1282 BCE), that mentions the battle. A detailed Hittite account has not yet been discovered (Redford 1992, 184).

The versions do not relate widely different accounts, but each version instead focuses on details that are sometimes missing in the other accounts. Egyptologists have carefully pieced together the different accounts of the battle, along with the pictorial representations, to produce a single narrative that details not just the dispositions and order of battle of both sides, but also the tactics they used (Breasted 2001, 126).

The Late Bronze Age

In ancient Egyptian history, between each of the three highpoints – the Old, Middle, and New Kingdoms – there were what modern historians refer to as "Intermediate Periods." Essentially, the Intermediate Periods were eras when the central authority diminished to the point that regional potentates assumed power, or as in the case of the Third Intermediate Period, the country was divided between foreign conquerors. During the Second Intermediate Period, which occurred between the Middle and New Kingdoms, the Delta region was ruled by a foreign power known as the Hyksos, while a native Egyptian dynasty ruled the remainder from the Upper Egyptian city of Thebes. This period is known today as the Seventeenth Dynasty.

The kings of the Seventeenth Dynasty consolidated their hold on southern Egypt until they were finally able to attack the Hyksos under the reigns of Seqenenre Tao (c. 1560 BCE) and Kamose (1555-1552 BCE). Although Ahmose I was Kamose's successor, Manetho considered him to be the progenitor of the Eighteenth Dynasty because he was the Egyptian king who eventually vanquished the Hyksos and drove them from Egypt. Ahmose I's battles with the Hyksos were depicted in pictorial reliefs that have been discovered at Abydos as well as in the tombs of his generals, Ahmose, son of Ibana and Ahmose Pennekhbet (Shaw and Nicholson 1995, 18). The text foreshadows a common Egyptian New Kingdom military tactic - the pharaoh fighting with his troops in a chariot - but the majority of the battle appears to have been ship-to-ship and ship-to-shore fighting.

Regardless, the final expulsion of the Hyksos was completed around the year 1540 BCE (Kuhrt 2010, 1:176), which marked the beginning of Egypt's 18th Dynasty, the New Kingdom, and its status as a Bronze Age imperial power among other kingdoms such as Hatti, Babylonia, and Assyria. The defeat of the Hyksos was probably accompanied by a major campaign into Nubia by the Egyptian army, which further solidified Egypt's status as an imperial power (Kemp 1983, 174).

Once the Hyksos were expelled from Egypt, the Egyptians were free to establish a new dynasty to rule over a once more unified Egypt, but the process did not take place overnight and was only possible after the Egyptians modernized their army.

Perhaps the most important hallmark of New Kingdom Egypt was its military. The Egyptian army of the New Kingdom thrust north into the Levant and south into Nubia to institute one of the world's first true empires and arguably the largest in the late Bronze Age. At the vanguard of the New Kingdom army and on every campaign was the pharaoh. The Egyptian concept of kingship did not change much during the New Kingdom compared to previous periods regarding divinity and other theological matters, but the king's role as a warrior and commander in chief became more pronounced and visible (Kuhrt 2010, 1:211). Primary sources, some of which will be explored more thoroughly below, indicate that the king's role as commander of the army was not ceremonial; he was expected to be an excellent charioteer and bowman. Military training was given to young crown princes in Memphis, and by all accounts the pharaohs-in-training took their schooling very seriously and even continued to hone their skills after ascending to the kingship. Eighteenth Dynasty king Amenhotep II (c. 1438-1412 BCE) saw his military duties as extremely important, even clearing away sand near the Sphinx to create a royal training and hunting grounds that he and several of his successors used (Kuhrt 2010, 1:213). The changes that took place in the Egyptian military during the late Second Intermediate Period and early New

Kingdom were not limited to the top, though; the entire military apparatus was drastically overhauled.

The fundamental difference that set the New Kingdom military apart from the Egyptian military in earlier periods was that it was a professional standing army. The army of the New Kingdom was no longer reliant on conscription to raise a suitable force for campaigns, and it was never short of well-trained professional warriors. At the core of the New Kingdom army was the chariot corps, who were the most able and best trained of all soldiers. The charioteers were nearly always life-long military members, and although they were culled from all classes of Egyptian society, they eventually formed their own elite class that was connected to the nobility (Kuhrt 2010, 1:217).

By the early part of the Eighteenth Dynasty, the military was already highly specialized, not unlike a modern army, with several different divisions and specialized units that included chariot corps, infantry, intelligence, supply, and designated naval units (Kuhrt 2010, 1:218). The Egyptian army of the New Kingdom also used weapons that its countrymen had not used in prior periods, including horses and chariots, compound bows, and new swords, all of which were imported from Asia (Spalinger 2005, 1-18). It was this highly advanced and complex army that drove the Hyksos from Egypt and then went on to conquer large parts of the Near East.

Kamose's successor, Ahmose (c. 1552-1527 BCE), is generally considered by modern scholars to be the first king of the Eighteenth Dynasty, marking his rule as the beginning of the New Kingdom. Although Ahmose still had to deal with remnants of the Hyksos in the Delta during the early part of his reign, he was free to set his sights on the Levant, particularly the city of Shauren, once he repelled those occupiers.

Ahmose's pursuit of the Hyksos into the Levant officially marks the beginning of the New Kingdom as Egypt expanded its borders to become an empire (Kuhrt 2010, 1:189). Ahmose followed up his northern campaign with expeditions into the south, which established Egyptian control over Nubia as far south as the second cataract (Kuhrt 2010, 1:190). The next couple of pharaohs followed up Ahmose's progress with even more forays into foreign lands.

Although Ahmose established the Eighteenth Dynasty and the New Kingdom, his successor, Amenhotep I (c. 1527-1507), instituted many of the salient features of New Kingdom culture. Perhaps the most important policy that Amenhotep I carried out was to bring the cult of the god Amun to prominence (Kuhrt 2010, 1:190). Before the New Kingdom, Amun was of more regional importance; he stood at the head of the pantheon in the Hermopolitan cosmology, but that creation myth was only one of three in ancient Egyptian theology. His popularity remained confined to the southern city of Thebes for the most part until Amenhotep I began to patronize the god's cult by giving generous amounts of war booty and taxes to Amun. Subsequent pharaohs followed this policy until Amun became the national god of Egypt and was even worshipped in foreign lands.

The Amarna Period and the Eighteenth Dynasty were followed by the Nineteenth and Twentieth Dynasties, which modern scholars collectively refer to as the "Ramesside Period." The period gets its name from two larger-than-life pharaohs named Ramesses, Ramesses II and Ramesses III, as well as the nine other pharaohs who also took that name.

The early part of the Ramesside Period was marked by a renewed, aggressive foreign policy in the Levant that put the Egyptians at odds with the ever-expanding Hittite Empire, while the latter part of the period saw a decline in Egypt's empire and wars against the Sea Peoples, Libyans, and Nubians just to retain the cohesion of their kingdom.

The Nineteenth Dynasty began with the reign of Ramesses I (c. 1306-1305), who was one of Horemheb's military colleagues. The throne then passed to Seti I (c. 1305-1290 BCE), who established many of the cultural hallmarks of the Ramesside Period. In terms of building projects, Seti I is credited with the construction of the Great Hypostyle Hall at Karnak, which served as the centerpiece of that great temple complex (Haeny 1997, 110). Seti I also built a mortuary temple near the Osiris temple at Abydos (Haney 1997, 112).

Seti I was also quite active in foreign affairs, campaigning in both the Levant and Nubia, but it would be his son and successor, Ramesses II (c. 1290-1224 BCE), who earned the greatest fame for his military endeavors.

A colossal statue depicting Ramesses II

The Great Powers Club

In terms of foreign policy, the first five years of Ramesses II's rule was spent conducting minor campaigns into Nubia and the Levant, which were meant to reestablish Egyptian dominance in those regions. The geopolitical situation had changed, though, during the Amarna Period, because the kingdom of Mitanni had collapsed, and in its place, the Assyrians established themselves as one of the "Great Powers" alongside the Egyptians, Babylonians, and Hittites. The Hittites also took advantage of the situation by conquering former Mitanni territory in Syria and making an aggressive push into the northern Levant. The Hittite King Muwatalli II (c. 1295-1272 BCE) led a campaign toward the major Canaanite city of Kadesh early in his reign (van de Mieroop 2007, 143). The precise reason for the Hittite offensive remains unknown, but it probably originated with the new Hittite king wanting to prove himself on the international scene and possibly a belief by the same king that his Egyptian counterpart was weak and inexperienced.

A depiction of Ramesses II firing arrows at the Nubians from his chariot

One of the more interesting developments of Egyptian history during the New Kingdom was the creation of a world order by the major kingdoms of the region, which modern scholars have come to know as the "Great Powers Club." The timeframe of the order roughly correlated with the early New Kingdom (ca. 1500-1200 BCE) and consisted the kingdoms of Egypt, Mittani, Hatti, and Babylon. Later, after Mitanni was destroyed, the kingdom of Assyria stepped in to take its place (van de Mieroop 2007, 129).

Essentially, the system was established to facilitate trade between the major powers and to avoid wars by demarcating the limits of their empires. Much of the inner workings of the system are known to modern scholars through a combination of documents discovered in each of the capital cities and a large cache of letters discovered in the Egyptian village of Amarna in the late 19th century, known today collectively as the "Amarna Letters." The Amarna Letters were written in the cuneiform script in the Akkadian language, which was the *lingua franca* of the Great Powers.

The letters reveal a two-tiered structure of correspondence that tells even more about the nature of the Great Powers system. The kings of the major powers would refer to each other as "brother," while the lesser powers, primarily the Canaanite city-states, were treated by the great kings as inferiors (van de Mieroop 2007, 134). The Canaanite city-states actually served as a buffer zone for the Great Powers, which used the small kingdoms as proxies to advance their imperialistic goals without having to risk a major engagement against another Great Power (van de Mieroop 2007, 134).

The correspondence between the various Egyptian kings and their counterparts provides a unique glimpse into the lives of late Bronze Age elites. When requesting commodities in the letters, the great kings would usually request items that were rare in their own countries but plentiful in the other. For instance, since Egypt had numerous gold and silver deposits at its disposal, the other kings often requested gold and silver. For their part, the Egyptian kings appeared to have favored foreign princesses as their favorite exotic commodity. In one particularly interesting letter, Tushratta, the king of Mitanni, sent one of his daughters to Amenhotep III in exchange for some rare items, including gold. The letter reads, "Tushratta of Mitanni sent his daughter, Kelu-Kehba, to Amenhotep III as a gift and as the greeting gift of Kelu-Kheba my sister, 1 set of gold toggle-pins, 1 set of gold (ear)rings, 1 gold *mashu*-ring 1 stone scent container full of fine oil. I am sending her." (Cochavi-Rainey 1999, 52).

Although the Egyptian kings coveted foreign princesses, they never sent their own women to foreign courts (van de Mieroop 2007, 138). The trade within the system moved in a counter-clockwise pattern beginning in Syria, moving to the Aegean region, then across the Mediterranean Sea to Egypt, and finally north from Egypt along the coastline into the Levant (van de Mieroop 2007, 140). The system began to fall apart during the reign of Ramesses II, but not before numerous transactions between the Egyptians and Hittites took place and were recorded.

Ramesses II even sent a gold-laden shipment specifically to the Hittite queen: "[The shipment which the great king, the king of the land of Egypt, has sent to the great king, the king of the land of Khatti and to the queen of the land of Khatti. 765 shekels of pure gold in ingots]. 1 . . . of pure gold set with a beautiful stone, its weight 234 shekels]. [1 . . . of pure gold set with a beautiful stone, its weight 83 shekels]. [10 drinking vessels of pure gold, their weight 480 shekels]. [1 *kaptukû*-vessel(?) of pure gold, its weight 96 shekels]. [x assorted "eyes" of gold inlaid, their weight 36 shekels]. [1 (necklace) for the neck, highly colored, of pure gold, its weight 26 shekels]. [1 pai[r of earrings of pure gold, its weight 22 shekels]. 11 rin[gs of pure gold, their weight 12 shekels.] 2 armbands [of pure gold with all kinds of stones, its weight 5 ½ shekels]. 1 chest." (Chochavi-Rainey 1999).

Other major regional states – including Elam in western Iran, the Myceneans, and the Anatolian state of Arzawa – were also major players, although they are not generally considered part of the "Great Powers" because they are rarely or never mentioned in the Amarna Letters archives.

The Campaign

Most major conflicts throughout history have taken place over one state's desire to acquire more territory or resources at the expense of another, or several states, and the main powers that existed during the Bronze Age were no different. The Canaanite states in the Levant served as a sort of buffer zone between Mitanni, Egypt, Babylon, and Hatti, with attacks or expeditions being conducted by major powers against the smaller states, but rarely against each other (Mieroop 2007, 134). The result was that by the late 14th century BCE, an ancient Cold War of sorts existed in the Near East, where the Great Powers would fund and instigate proxies in the

Levant to go to war against the proxies of other geopolitical adversaries. Alliances were made between the Great Powers, but as a letter from Burnaburish II of Babylon (c. 1359-1333 BCE) to an Egyptian king, probably Akhenaten (c. 1364-1347 BCE) demonstrated, those alliances were tenuous in the Levant: "In the time of Kurigalzu, my ancestor, all the Canaanites wrote here to him, saying, 'C[om]e to the border of the country so we can revolt and be allied [wi]the you.' My ancestor sent them this (reply), saying, 'Forget about being allied with me. If you become enemies of the king of Egypt, and are allied with anyone else, will I not then come and plunder you? How can there be an alliance with me?' For the sake of your ancestor my ancestor did not listen to them." (Moran 1992, 18)

As that letter was being written, though, the Hittites were making major moves to disrupt the system. In fact, the Hittites were preparing to flex their muscles at the expense of Mitanni and Egypt, putting the powers on a trajectory to meet in battle at Kadesh.

The Hittites occupied the mountainous region of central Anatolia, building a capital city there and naming in Hattusa. The Hittites were landlocked and had to rely on ports they later conquered for sea travel, which posed obvious problems (Macqueen 2003, 39). On the other hand, the mountains protected Hatti and Hattusa from major attacks, and it was rich in tin and other materials (Macqueen 2003, 43).

The prospects of the Hittite Empire ebbed and flowed, as was the case with most Bronze Age empires in the Near East. Most notably, the Hittite Empire experienced a collapse that lasted for about 70 years before finally ending with the accession of King Telepinu (c. 1525-1500 BCE). Telepinu brought political stability back to Hatti, but it was Tudhaliya I (ruled c. 1430-1420) who modern scholars view as the father of the Hittite New Kingdom or New Empire (Kuhrt 2010, 244).

The landlocked Hittites wasted no time expanding from Hattusa into Arzawa, Mitanni, and eventually Egyptian territories. The Hittite King Suppiluliuma I (c. 1370-1330 BCE) was a particularly vigorous ruler when it came to martial endeavors, first retaking lost lands in Anatolia and then turning south into Mitanni lands (Macqueen 2003, 46). Many Hittite leaders demonstrated sophisticated political acumen, and Suppiluliuma especially knew how to work the Great Powers to his advantage, using a combination of diplomacy and warfare to slowly expand Hittite territory south into the Levant at Mitanni's expense. Hatti's campaign against Mitanni weakened the latter so much that the Hittites were able to sack the Mitanni capital of Wassukani and take most of the decaying empire's possessions in the northern Levant (Redford 1992, 174). The Assyrians would quickly fill the vacuum left by the destroyed Mitanni state, but in the late 14th century, the Hittites were only concerned with the Egyptians in the southern Levant.

There are no documents that indicate a direct conflict between the Hittites and Egyptians during the reign of Suppiluliuma, or during the reigns of Akhenaten, Smenkhara, and Tutankhamun (c. 1345-1335 BCE) (Schulman 1978, 44). This is not to say that the Amarna kings did not conduct military expeditions into the Levant (there are pictorial reliefs that suggest they did), but none depict a direct confrontation with the Hittites (Kuhrt 2010, 196-7). It appears that both sides continued to utilize their Canaanite proxies in the Levant to jockey for position instead of fighting each other directly. If so, it was likely that the Hittites and Egyptians were content not to upset the status quo, which a direct confrontation could have threatened

Somewhat ironically, it seems a diplomatic incident heightened tensions between the two powers. Hittite sources suggest that Tutankhamun's widow, Ankhesenamun, sent a letter to Suppiluliuma requesting a prince for her to marry (Dijk 2000, 292). This was a most unusual request because, as mentioned earlier, the Egyptians never gave their princesses to foreigners, even other Great Powers (Schulman 1979). Suppiluliuma was rightfully suspicious of the request, relating his suspicions as well as the queen's letter in a cuneiform text: "While my father was down in the country of Karkamis, he dispatched Lupakkis and Tessub-zalmas to the country of Amqa. They proceeded to attack the country of Amqa and brought deportees, cattle (and) sheep home before my father. When the people of the land of Egypt heard about the attack on Amqa, they became frightened. Because, to make matters worse, their lord Bibhururiyas had just died, the Egyptian queen who had become a widow, sent an envoy to my father and wrote him as follows: 'My husband died and I have no son. People say that you have many sons. If you were to send me one of your sons, he might become my husband. I am loath to take a servant of mine and make him my husband.' . . . When my father heard that, he called the great into council . . . 'Perhaps they have a prince; they may try to deceive me and do not really want one of my sons to (take over) the kingship,' the Egyptian queen answered my father in a letter as follows: Why do you say: 'They may try to deceive me'? If I had a son, would I write to a foreign country in a manner which is humiliating to myself and my country?" (Pritchard 1992, 319).

The Hittite king's counselors no doubt advised him to be weary and some probably told him to ignore the pleas altogether, but after apparently believing the Egyptian queen to be honest, and perhaps seeing a political opportunity, he sent his son Zananza with a military force to confirm the marriage in person.

Suppiluliuma was certainly a wise and shrewd king, as evidenced by the fact he lived so long and conquered so many foes, so he should have followed his initial instinct on the matter. The supposed diplomatic marriage turned into armed conflict when the two forces met, ending in tragedy for the Hittite royal family. According to the "Plague Prayer" of Hittite King Mursili II (c. 1330-1295 BCE), the Hittites actually attacked first: "My father sent foot soldiers and charioteers who attacked the country of Amka, Egyptian territory. Again he sent troops, and again they attacked it. When the Egyptians became frightened, they asked outright for one of his sons to (take over) the kingship. But when my father gave them one of his sons, they killed him as they led him there." (Pritchard, 1992, 395).

The details of how and why Zananza was assassinated are unclear, but it likely had to do with the political complexities in Egypt during the period, as Ay (c. 1335-1332 BCE) was nominally on the throne and General Horemheb (c. 1332-1306 BCE) would come after him. Neither of those two men could have wanted the queen to marry a Hittite prince. The battle was indecisive, but the Hittites brought a plague back to Hatti that likely killed Suppiluliuma and his successor, Arnuwanda II, who only ruled in 1330 BCE (Kuhrt 2010, 254).

Whatever the details of the "Zananza Affair," it left relations between the Hittites and Egyptians badly damaged. When Mursili II came to the Hittite throne, he continued Suppiluliuma's aggressive policy in the Levant, and he was immediately challenged by Seti I. The kings clashed, but they apparently determined that the border clashes were too costly, so they came to an agreement to not encroach on each other's spheres of influence in the Levant, even though the precise division of the empires is still unclear (Redford 1992, 182-3). It may have been that the treaty was never put into writing, which led to ambiguities concerning allegiances that the Canaanite princes were happy to exploit.

 Mursili was succeeded by Muwatalli II (c. 1295-1272 BCE) and Seti by Ramesses II, and, despite their cultural differences, the two young rulers were very similar in many ways. Both men were aggressive military campaigners who were attempting to prove themselves to their own people as they rose to power. At the same time, since both rulers were deeply connected to the military establishments in their respective kingdoms thanks to their fathers, they were probably expected to make a name for themselves militarily not long after coming to power, or at least they believed it necessary.

 Muwatalli almost immediately disregarded the agreement his predecessor made with Seti by campaigning in the Levant and instigating Canaanite princes in Egyptian-claimed territory to rebel against their overlords. The Hittite king's campaign was likely due to the king of Amurru switching his allegiance from Hatti to Egypt towards the end of Seti I's rule (Redford 1992, 183). Ramesses II led a full military expedition to Amurru in his fourth year of rule, possibly to personally accept the Amurru king's obeisance. Inevitably, Muwatalli viewed the turn of events as a personal affront and a threat to his power, so he began a military expedition of his own (Redford 1992, 183).

 After his successful campaign to Amurru, Ramesses returned to Egypt as a victorious pharaoh, but, like Muwatalli, also made plans to return to the region. In the fifth year of his rule, Ramesses left Egypt with four divisions – likely the majority of Egypt's standing army at the time – and marched across the Levant for about three weeks before arriving in Kadesh, Syria (Spalinger 2005, 212). The goal of Ramesses' second military campaign remains a bit of a mystery, but it was likely to bring Kadesh into the Egyptian fold since it bordered Amurru and was in an area hotly contested by the Egyptians and Hittites (Manley 1996, 93).

 It is possible that Ramesses expected his second campaign to go much like the first, which would have meant he never directly encountered the Hittites (Spalinger 2005, 211). At the same time, however, the force he led was the largest in recorded history up to that point, so it is also likely that he expected to face some stiff resistance, whether from the Hittites or the Canaanite princes.

The Egyptian and Hittite armies were both quintessential Late Bronze Age militaries in many ways, employing several of the same tactics and most of the same weapons, although there were some notable differences. The technology both empires had access to at the time was virtually the same, but they did choose to utilize those technologies in slightly different ways.

Chariots formed the backbone of both armies and were used by the nobility and elites. Hittite chariots, though, were slightly different than their Egyptian counterparts and were also utilized slightly differently. Hittite chariots consisted of a wooden frame that was covered by leather, and the axle was attached to the middle of the body rather than the rear as they were on Egyptian chariots, which made them bigger and heavier (Macqueen 2003, 57). The disadvantage of this design was that the chariots were slower and less maneuverable than their Egyptian counterparts, but they had the advantage of being able to hold three men – a driver, a shield bearer, and a spear thrower – instead of the two men an Egyptian chariot could hold (Macqueen 2003, 58). Chariots usually led an attack, and once the fighting commenced in earnest, the infantry would enter the fray.

Hittite infantry fought in a tight phalanx formation with long spears, and if the phalanx was broken, the soldiers would use daggers (Macqueen 2003, 59). The armor used by Hittite and Egyptian infantry usually consisted of a leather sleeveless jacket that was worn over a corselet that was possibly bronze (Macqueen 2003, 63). Although the chariot corps had better resources due to their higher status, chariot warriors needed less armor because a shield bearer accompanied every driver for both the Egyptians and Hittites, and too much armor would hamper a driver's or spear thrower's effectiveness.

Pictorial reliefs from Egypt depict the Egyptian chariot drivers using bows, suggesting it was an elite weapon in that kingdom, although it appears that only light infantry used bows in the Hittite army (Macqueen 2003, 61). The reliefs also seem to indicate that unlike the Egyptians, the Hittites did not use composite bows (Spalinger 2005, 217).

One final unit of the Hittite military worth mentioning are the so-called *teher* warriors. The word *teher* is actually an ancient Egyptian word, used in the Kadesh inscriptions to describe the elite warrior bodyguards who surrounded Muwatalli during the battle (Spalinger 2005, 217). Little more is known about the *teher,* and the word itself is translated in modern Egyptian-English dictionaries as "Syrian warriors," although their ethnicity cannot be positively determined (Faulkner 1999, 301).

Egyptian chariot drivers had to be a bit more skilled than their Hittite opponents because they fought with bows in addition to driving (Spalinger 2005, 18). The manner in which Egyptian chariot drivers maneuvered their vehicles and fired bows at the same time was obviously complicated and depended on the situation. There were situations when the charioteers would drive close to the enemy force, stop, and then begin shooting. This could be done against enemy infantry, but when the enemy employed a sizable chariot corps, it would not suffice. Numerous reliefs from Egypt depict Ramesses, as well as other pharaohs, shooting while their chariot is moving by attaching the reigns to a holder on their waist (Spalinger 2005, 18-19). It has been debated by modern experts whether this was a tactic used in war or for hunting, with Spalinger suggesting that evidence for this is only circumstantial since it is based on pictorial reliefs (Spalinger 2005, 18). Egyptian chariots were also equipped with a number of javelins/spears kept in a sheath on the side of the chariot. The javelins were thrown by the spear bearer, probably if the charioteer was out of arrows or in situations where the driver needed to have both hands on the reigns, such as a charger or retreat (Spalinger 2005, 19).

In a standard battle, such as at Kadesh, the chariot corps would lead the fight against the enemy's chariot corps, which was then supported by the infantry.

Perhaps the most notable element of the Egyptian infantry depicted in pictorial reliefs from the New Kingdom is its use of the distinct "sickle swords." Named for the notable curved shape, these bronze swords were meant for slashing and hacking attacks more than stabbing, as with conventional swords. Although the sickle sword, or *khepish* as the Egyptians knew it, has come to be associated with Egypt, they were used throughout the Near East in the Late Bronze Age (Spalinger 2005, 17).

Modern scholars also know more about the Egyptians' use of armor thanks to the pictorial reliefs. The shields were simple; wood covered by leather (Spalinger 2005, 16). The Egyptian soldiers wore the same armor as their Hittite foes, with the charioteers wearing less, as mentioned earlier. Although the sickle sword was effective and was a step up from earlier daggers and swords, it was the invention and diffusion of the composite bow throughout the Near East that led to armies using leather and bronze armor (Spalinger 2005, 15). When the two armies met at Kadesh, they therefore looked quite similar and used most of the same weapons, but the Egyptians had two distinct units that played an important role.

Like Muwatalli, Ramesses also had an elite guard that surrounded him, and a bit more is known about his. They are identified in texts and pictorial representations as the Sherden/Shardana, who, curiously, were among the Sea Peoples that later ravaged much of the eastern Mediterranean, including Egypt. The origins of the Sherden remain a mystery, although it is believed by many scholars that the name indicates either a Sardinian origin, or that they settled in Sardinia after their Late Bronze Age migrations (Cline and O'Connor 2003, 112). Ramesses II's use of the Sherden as his elite guard was first documented at the Battle of Kadesh, and it was likely that they were mercenaries (Redford 1992, 243). In the pictorial representations, the Sherden are notably different than the standard Egyptian infantry: Sherden warriors carry round shields, long swords that are wide at the haft, and distinct helmets that have two prongs and a small sphere in the middle (Spalinger 2005, 209). The Sherden were always depicted as foot soldiers, never in chariots, and always close to the king, similar to the *teher* warriors. The Sherden and *teher* raise at least one interesting question about the Battle of Kadesh and the nature of the Egyptian and Hittite militaries in general. The use of elite guards is not especially unique, but the fact that the Sherden were clearly foreign and the *teher* were possibly not ethnic Hittites leads one to wonder why the kings could not find elite bodyguards among their own people.

Another unit the Egyptians employed at Kadesh that merits some attention was known as the Na'arn. The Na'arn comprised the fifth division in Ramesses' army at Kadesh – although it is not known how large the unit was, so referring to it as a division may be a bit arbitrary – and played an important role in the late stages of the battle, but identifying them has been a bit problematic. The Na'arn arrived at the Battle of Kadesh from the north, separate from the four Egyptian divisions, indicating that they traveled alone to the location. One theory is that the Na'arn traveled from the Egyptian garrison in Gaza by sea, debarked in Amurru, and then marched south to Kadesh (Manley 1996, 93). This would explain why the Na'arn arrived at Kadesh separate from the other Egyptian divisions, but it does not explain the background of the unit and what their specialty was. It is believed that the Na'arn were an elite infantry unit that was stationed in the southern Levant, likely specializing in putting down rebellions in the Canaanite city-states. Many modern scholars believe the Na'arn were elite foreign warriors and translate the term as "an independent body of Asiatic warriors" or "high warrior class" (Lesko 2002, 229). Although it does seem likely that the Na'arn were native Canaanites, it is also possible they were ethnic Egyptians permanently stationed in the Levant (Spalinger 2005, 7). The Na'arn may have simply adopted a non-Egyptian look and style, much as Zouaves did in the French military in the 19th century.

Determining the order of battle at Kadesh in a modern sense of the term is difficult for a few reasons, the most obvious being the lack of a Hittite source that details the size and disposition of the Hittite army. In the same vein, even though the Egyptian sources do give scholars a general sense of the size and disposition of the Egyptian army, they are lacking in specific details. Egyptologists have based their estimates of the size of the Egyptian army based on some references in the texts as well as the pictorial representations, while estimates of the Hittite army are based on Egyptian references. There is a fair amount of range in the total number of men who fought at Kadesh, although all modern experts agree that the overall number was quite large, and likely the largest that two armies had put on the same field up until that time.

Today, historians believe the total numbers of soldiers involved in the Battle of Kadesh on both sides numbered around 40,000 men, roughly divided equally between Egyptian and Hittite (Breasted 2001, 127). Arriving at the number of the Hittite forces is difficult because only one number is given in the accounts of the battle, which was a reference to the battalion used in the initial attack. It is also important to point out that the Hittites used more native Canaanites in the battle than the Egyptians did, although in the pictorial reliefs they are clearly marked (Breasted 2001, 129). Thus, historians have to rely on the numbers of the Egyptian army to estimate the size of the Hittite force. It is believed that the size of an Egyptian division was about 5,000 men, and there were four divisions and the Na'arn, putting the total number at around 20,000 (Spalinger 2005, 216).

When the Egyptians marched into Kadesh, they did so in a formation that was well-documented in the textual and pictorial sources. The four Egyptian divisions were named for the most important gods during the Nineteenth Dynasty– Amun, Ra/Pre, Ptah, and Seth/Sutekh – with the Amun division being the one Ramesses led. As such, that division would also lead the march from Egypt to Kadesh. The pictorial representations show that each division was equipped and marched similarly, with the chariots leading the march. The reliefs also depict each division marching with some distance between each other, but the order and distance can only be determined from the texts. The texts relate that the Ramesses and the Amun divisions marched into Kadesh first, followed by the Ra division, then the Ptah division, and finally the Seth division. As will be further discussed below, once the battle began, the Amun, Ra, and Na'arn divisions were engaged in the majority of the fighting, while the Ptah division arrived late and the Seth division may not have been involved in any fighting, at least on the first day. This indicates that each division marched with considerable distance between each other, perhaps several miles (Spalinger 2005, 212).

Since the Hittites and their Canaanite allies concealed themselves to the east of Kadesh before the battle, and because no detailed Hittite account of the battle has so far been discovered, it is virtually impossible to determine the Hittite order of battle just prior to the fighting. The account of the battle indicates that the army was orderly, and, as has already been discussed, it was comprised of different specialists. The Kadesh inscriptions enumerate the different Canaanite states involved the battle, with "Kheta" being Breasted's translation of "Hatti" or "Land of the Hittites." "The wretched, vanquished chief of Kheta had come, having gathered together all countries from the ends of the sea to the land of Kheta, which came entire: the Naharin likewise, and Arvad, ____, Mesa, Keshkesh, Kelekesh, Luka, Kezweden, Carchemish, Ekereth, Kode, the entire land of Nuges, Mesheneth, and Kadesh." (Breasted 2001, 138).

Based on this information, one can assume that the Hittite army at Kadesh was also divided into divisions, but because there were so many different Canaanite states present, the divisions of the Hittite army were either smaller than the Egyptian army or multiple Canaanite states were grouped together to form a full division.

The Battle of Kadesh

The Orontes River was the point of no return for the Egyptian army, because once they crossed this small, shallow river, the city of Kadesh was to the northeast of their march on a plain. Before they got to Kadesh, though, they had to ford the Orontes near an otherwise insignificant village named Shabtuna. It was here that the battle truly began in many ways when two Shasu tribesmen approached the Egyptians claiming they and their people were prepared to switch sides in the absence of the Hittite king: "When the king proceeded northward, and his majesty had arrived at the locality south of the town of Shabtuna, there came two Shasu, to speak to his majesty as follows: 'Our brethren, who belong to the greatest of the families with the vanquished chief of Kheta, have made us come to his majesty, to say: 'We will be subjects of Pharaoh . . . for the vanquished chief of Kheta sits in the land of Aleppo, on the north of Tunip.'' Now, these Shasu spake these words, which they spake to his majesty, falsely, (for) the vanquished chief of Kheta made them come to spy where his majesty was, in order to cause the army of his majesty not to draw up for fighting him, to battle with the vanquished chief of Kheta." (Breasted 2001, 144).

The passage reveals that Muwatalli was one step ahead of Ramesses in the intelligence game. Espionage is often thought of as a purely modern ancillary to warfare, but this example shows that Muwatalli knew the importance of espionage and intelligence, and he also knew how valuable planting false intelligence could be.

Believing that the gods had favored him with the intelligence report, Ramesses moved forward with the Amun division far in front of the other three divisions. As Ramesses and the Amun division marched to a position in front of Kadesh to its northwest, they made camp and waited for the other three divisions to arrive, unaware that the Hittites and their allies were on the other side of the city: "Behold, the wretched, vanquished of Kheta, together with the numerous allied countries, were stationed in battle array, concealed on the northeast of the city of Kadesh, while his majesty was alone by himself, [with] his bodyguard, and the division of Amon was marching behind him. The division of Re crossed over the river-bed on the south side of the town of Shabtuna, at the distance of an iter from the [division of Amon]; _______ the division of Ptah was on the south of the city of Aranami; and the division of Sutekh was marching upon the road." (Breasted 2001, 139).

This part of the account is quite useful to determine the locations of the armies as the battle began, with the Hittites (Kheta) concealed northeast of Kadesh, while Ramesses and the Amun division were to the northwest (Manley 1996, 93). Unaware of what awaited him on the other side of Kadesh, Ramesses II and his division made camp, and the Kadesh inscriptions describe Ramesses and the Amun division relaxing as they set up camp, almost acting nonchalantly: "When the two Shosu who were in the Presence had been [released], his majesty proceeded northward and reached the northwest of Kadesh. The camp of his majesty's army was pitched there, and his majesty took his seat on a throne of fine gold to the north of Kadesh on the west side of the Orontes."

The passage brings back the question posed earlier over what Ramesses II's intentions were. The seemingly calm attitude portrayed in the texts seems to suggest that the Egyptian king never thought he would encounter the formidable Hittite army. Spalinger has suggested that Ramesses II was possibly preparing to fight only the army of Kadesh the following day on the plain to the west of the city (Spalinger 2005, 213). If this theory is true, Ramesses probably believed he could take Kadesh with only the Amun and Ra divisions, but if need be he had the Ptah, Seth, and Na'arn divisions waiting.

However, as the pharaoh and the Amun division were relaxing and preparing for a battle the next day, a more accurate intelligence report was brought to the camp. Although Ramesses believed the initial false intelligence report of the Hittite's movements, he was still prepared enough to send his own scouts to search the other side of Kadesh. When the scouts returned, they informed the pharaoh that he was facing a potentially deadly situation: "Then came a scout who was in his majesty's retinue bringing two scouts of the Foe from Khati. When they had been brought into the Presence, his majesty said to them: 'What are you?' They said: 'We belong to the Chief of Khatti. It is he who sent us to observe where his majesty is.' His majesty said to them: 'Where is he, the Foe from Khatti' I have heard he is in the land of Khaleb to the north of Tunip.' They said to his majesty: 'Look, the vile Chief of Khatti has come together with the many countries who are with him, whom he has brought with him as allies, the land of Dardany, the land of Nahrin, that of Keushkesh, those of Masa, those of Pidasa, the land of Karkisha and Luka, the land of Carchemish, the land of Arzawa, the land of Ugarit, that of Irun, the land of Inesa, Mushanet, Kadesh, Khaleb, and the entire land of Kedy. They are equipped with their infantry and their chariotry, and with their weapons of war. They are more numerous than the sands of the shores. Look, they stand equipped and ready to fight behind Kadesh the Old.'" (Lichtheim 1976, 60-61).

It is undoubtedly untrue that the captured Hittite scouts referred to their king as the "vile chief of Hatti," but the rest of the account is likely accurate. The turn of events placed Ramesses in an extremely precarious position, as the Ra division was still more than a half day's march from Kadesh, and the Ptah and Seth divisions were still south of the Orontes River (Spalinger 2005, 210-12).

The pharaoh immediately sought consul with his generals. Many people today believe that kings and emperors in the pre-modern era were complete authoritarians who did what they pleased and imprisoned or killed any of their subordinates who questioned them. This idea is probably more the result of modern dictatorships than reality, because successful rulers often took the advice of those closest to them, especially when the advisors were experts in their fields. Although there is no doubt Ramesses was an authoritarian, he also lived a long life, had a long, stable rule, and likely learned much by watching his father. The Egyptian sources indicate that he was wise enough to ask others' opinions: "Lo, while his majesty sat talking with the princes, the vanquished chief of Kheta came, and the numerous countries, which were with him. They crossed over the channel on the south of Kadesh, and charged into the army of his majesty while they were marching, and not expecting it." (Breasted 2001, 146-7).

Unfortunately, the texts do not relate the advice the generals gave Ramesses, or if they even had the chance to do so, because Muwatalli's attack immediately changed the course of the campaign, seizing the initiative from the Egyptians and forcing them into a defenseive position. When the Hittites struck, the Ra division was just southwest of Kadesh, the Ptah division was fording the Orontes, and the Seth division was still south of the river. The Hittites and their allies emerged from behind Kadesh, but, instead of attacking the Amun camp, they went for the Ra division: "Then they came forth from the south side of Kadesh and attacked the army of Pre in its middle, as they were marching unaware and not prepared to fight. Then the infantry and chariotry of his majesty weakened before them, while his majesty was stationed to the north of the town of Kadesh, on the west bank of the Orontes." (Lichtheim 1976, 64).

It is important to note that the Orontes River flows north to south past what was the west side of Kadesh before bending at Shabtuna to a more southwesterly direction, so the Hittites had to ford the river in order to attack the Ra division. The Hittite attack threw the Ra division into disarray and threatened the Amun division and the pharaoh himself, but according to the Kadesh inscriptions, instead of retreating, Ramesses personally led a counterattack: "His majesty halted in the rout; then he charged into the foe, the vanquished of Kheta, being alone by himself and none other with him. When his majesty went to look behind him, he found 2,500 chariotry surrounding him, in his way out, being all the youth of the wretched Kheta, together with its numerous allied countries." (Breasted 2001, 141).

The 2,500 Hittite chariots mentioned is the first text that relates a tangible number of the Hittite force's size. The number is certainly reasonable if one accepts that Egyptian divisions were approximately 5,000 men. It is likely that Muwatalli sent a shock force for the initial attack, but the number cannot be totally trusted because it is only mentioned in the Egyptian sources (Spalinger 2005, 215). It is possible that the Hittite force was smaller and the Egyptian chroniclers inflated the numbers to make Ramesses look more heroic, but it is likelier that the Egyptian chroniclers made an estimate based on the size of the divisions in their own army.

It makes sense that the pharaoh personally charged and was surrounded, but he made sure to fictionalize what happened to him next. The most dramatic element of the Battle of Kadesh, and the part that has the most "added layers" in the texts, is the pharaoh being left alone in the midst of the initial attack. During the initial confusion of Muwatalli's attack, it appears the Hittite king may also have been alone for a period of time, but it was Ramesses II's experience that was memorialized and survived for posterity. His predicament was detailed in the "poem," although a critical reading of the text has been a source of debate among historians – after all, since Ramesses made incredible claims about slaying thousands of Hittites by himself, the text cannot be read literally, even though it does appear to follow some historical facts. The poem is also important due to the pharaoh's incredulous and almost sacrilegious stance towards the Egyptian gods.

By piecing together the historical and the more literary elements of the poem, historians think they have developed a clearer picture of the battle's chaos in the early stage. It appears that once the Hittites attacked the Ra division, the pharaoh ordered a counterattack that was unsuccessful, probably due to the initial confusion caused by the Hittite attack. Ramesses explained these facts early in the poem: "I charged all countries, while I was alone, my infantry and my chariotry having forsaken me. Not one among them stood to turn about. I swear, as Re loves me, as my father, Atum, favors me, that as for every matter which his majesty has stated, I did it in truth, in the presence of my infantry and my chariotry." (Breasted 2001, 147).

Although the focus of that passage is that the gods should realize Ramesses' piety, the factual information indicates that the king was not only surrounded, but was also without his trusty chariot. The Kadesh texts do not indicate precisely how it happened, but one can draw the conclusion that as the battle raged, Ramesses fell from his chariot and suddenly found himself surrounded by the Hittites and their Canaanite allies. Ramesses could not have been truly alone or he would have been killed or captured, but he likely felt as much as he looked around and had to fight his way back to the camp. Since Ramesses was a charioteer, he was armed with a bow, not a sword, which would have made his escape from the encirclement much more difficult. The pharaoh likely had to grab a discarded sword and fight his way out of the predicament.

The poem then relates that Ramesses fought the enemies by himself, without offering any details about how he was able to achieve such a fantastic feat:

> "He of Dardany, the chief of Carchemish,
>
> The chief of Karkisha, he of Khaleb,
>
> The brothers of him of Khatti all together,
>
> Their total of a thousand chariots came straight into the fire.
>
> I charged toward them, being like Mont,
>
> In a moment I have them a taste of my hand,
>
> I slaughtered among them, they were slain on the spot." (Lichtheim 1976, 67)

Ramesses clearly did not slay 1,000 charioteers, but underneath the hyperbole readers can get a sense of the desperate situation he faced. The reference to 1,000 charioteers also indicates a second Hittite attack after the first one led by 2,500 chariots failed (Spalinger 2005, 214). Since the pictorial reliefs often show the Sherden near Ramesses, it is reasonable to assume that at least a few of the Sherden were in the vicinity to help usher the Egyptian king to safety.

What's shocking is that the descriptions of the battle forsake the gods. The fact that the gods were mentioned in a text is not remarkable, but Ramesses' almost profane statements toward the gods is what makes the text unique. In one specific passage, Ramesses singles out Amun, the namesake of his division and the national god of Egypt during the New Kingdom:

"No officer was with me, no charioteer,

No soldier of the army, no shield-bearer;

My infantry, my chariotry yielded before them,

Not one of them stood firm to fight with them.

His majesty spoke: 'What is this, father Amun?

Is it right for a father to ignore his son?

Are my deeds a matter for you to ignore?

Do I not walk and stand at your word?

I have not neglected an order you gave.

Too great is he, the great lord of Egypt,

To allow aliens to step on his path!

What are these Asiatics to you, O Amun,

The wretches ignorant of god?

Have I not made for you many great monuments,

Filled your temple with my booty,

Built for you my mansion of Millions-of-Years,

Given you all my wealth as endowment?'" (Lichtheim 1976, 65).

The passage, and several others like it in the poem, contain a mix of frustration and grandiosity on the part of Ramesses. The king was clearly outmaneuvered and losing, which he blamed on the gods, but the fact that he even felt himself on the same level as the gods that he could refer to them in such a way is a sign of his immense ego. After all, Ramesses, like other Egyptian kings, was considered divine.

Muwatalli probably hoped for a quick victory over the Amun and Ra divisions, ensuring that by the time the Ptah and Seth divisions arrived, the battle would be over and Ramesses would be a captive. Based on how well Muwatalli utilized intelligence before the battle, it is likely he knew about the Ptah and Seth divisions to the south and therefore decided that striking the Amun and Ra divisions before the other two divisions crossed the Orontes River was optimal. Muwatalli, though, must have underestimated the Amun and Ra divisions' capabilities because he did not send enough men to finish them off, and as Ramesses and the other Egyptians fought for their survival, reinforcements finally arrived. The Na'arn warriors arrived on the battlefield from a coastal location in the land of Amur, where they were apparently being held in reserve but quite possibly tired from a long march: "And his majesty had made a first battle force from the best of his army, and it was on the shore of the land of Amor." (Lichtheim 1976, 64).

These were the elite Na'arn warriors, who were likely transported by sea from their garrison in Gaza in the southern Levant to Egyptian-claimed Amur in the northern Levant (Manley 1996, 93). The Na'arn arrived at the battle from the north of the Egyptian camp just in time and were able to blunt the Hittite attack: "The arrival of the recruits of Pharaoh, L.P.H., from the land of Amor. They found that the force of the vanquished chief of Kheta had surrounded the camp of his majesty on its western side. His majesty had been camping alone, no army with him, [awaiting the] arrival of his [officers] and his army and the division with which Pharaoh, L.PH., was, had not finished setting up the camp. . . Then the recruits cut off the foe belonging to the vanquished chief of Kheta, while they (the foe) were entering into the camp, and Pharaoh's officers slew them; they left not a single survivor among them." (Breasted 2001, 155).

The arrival of the Na'arn quickly turned the tide of the battle and gave the initiative to the Egyptians. Muwatalli sent another wave of chariots to attack the Egyptian camp, but the arrival of the Na'arn, combined with the approaching arrival of the Ptah and Seth divisions, meant that he no longer had the numbers to destroy the Egyptian army (Spalinger 2005, 226). Once the Hittites were pushed back, both sides had a respite until at least the next day.

What happened next at the Battle of Kadesh is a source of debate among modern historians. Some, such as Spalinger, believe there was a second day of fighting (Spalinger 2005, 217). This is certainly logical when one considers the nature of warfare in the ancient world. Fighting rarely took place after sundown, so if a battle was indecisive after the first day and both sides still had plenty of men, the two armies would often meet the following day to settle things decisively. The poem does appear to corroborate the argument that fighting commenced on the second day:

"At dawn I marshaled the ranks for battle,

I was ready to fight like an eager bull;

I arose against them in the likeness of Mont,

Equipped with my weapons of victory.

I charged their ranks fighting as a falcon pounces,

The serpent on my brow felled my foes,

Cast her fiery breath in my enemies' faces,

I was like Re when he rises at dawn." (Lichtheim 1976, 70).

The reference to Ramesses marshalling his troops at dawns appears to be the best indicator of a second day of fighting, because Muwatalli's initial attack came just after the Amun division made camp after a march. With that said, there are arguments that the battle ended after the first day. The poem is the only text to suggest there may have been more fighting, and even that reference is fleeting and ambiguous. The fact that scribes dedicated several different versions of the battle, and they were inscribed on the walls of multiple temples, demonstrates how important Ramesses II and the Egyptians in general believed the battle was, so one would think that the texts would be clearer about a second day of fighting. Still, it must also be pointed out that such a detailed record of a battle was a new concept and that Egyptian historiography as a discipline was quite different than modern historiography. It was not until the 4th century BCE that Egyptian historical texts were specifically written to describe a period of the past for the writer's contemporaries, and even then the texts were often meant to associate the subject with the divine.

From a military standpoint, the Battle of Kadesh was a tactical victory for the Egyptians but a strategic victory for the Hittites. The Kadesh inscriptions all indicate that despite suffering a costly initial attack, the Egyptians recovered enough to win the battle. According to Redford, Muwatalli had over 10,000 infantry that he never used, possibly thinking that the initial attack of 2,500 chariots would be adequate (Redford 1992, 185).

Either way, as glorious as the inscriptions portray Ramesses' victory at Kadesh, it was in every sense a Pyrrhic victory. The number of Egyptian dead is never related in the Kadesh inscriptions – as it would not have been by the very nature of Egyptian historiography – but it was likely high. The Ra division was probably devastated and needed to be replenished, and the Amun division also suffered significant losses. The Hittites also sustained massive casualties in the battle, but they were able to maintain their long-term position in the region.

There is no doubt that that Battle of Kadesh did not result in the desired outcome for Muwatalli. The Hittite king hoped to decimate at least the Amun and Ra divisions, if not the entire Egyptian army, and capture or kill Ramesses. Pictorial reliefs and texts from the Karnak Temple in Thebes, Egypt, reveal that the results were nearly the opposite. One relief depicts four of Ramesses II's sons leading lines of prisoners, who are listed as the "chiefs of Hatti." The text further claims, "Captives from the northern countries, who came to overthrow his majesty, whom his majesty slew, and whose subjects he brought as living captives, to fill the storehouse of his father, Amon." (Breasted 2001, 157) .

The captions accompanying the reliefs also indicate the status of a few of the dead Hittites. Among the dead Hittites were troop-captains, a shield bearer, and two *teher* commanders, indicating that the Hittites probably suffered as many, if not more losses than the Egyptians, and some of the losses were among their elites (Spalinger 2005, 226). Still, the Hittites remained on the field after the fighting and the pharaoh led his army back south through territory in the Levant that was firmly in Egyptian hands. Once back in Egypt, the pharaoh had to rebuild what was left of his army and was virtually powerless to stop any Hittite activity in the northern Levant. The Hittites wasted little time taking back the kingdom of Amurru and bringing its king, Benteretire, in chains to Hatti (Redford 1992, 185).

Ramifications

The effects of the battle would be felt in the Near East for several decades, which makes sense given that the Battle of Kadesh was the first major battle in history to be so thoroughly documented. Although both the Egyptians and Hittites would go on to fight in many other battles, the two sides never again engaged each other in a major battle. The end of direct conflict between them meant that the two empires could focus on consolidating their colonial possessions and refocusing their geopolitical activities on diplomacy instead of warfare.

Months after the Battle of Kadesh, the Canaanite city-states of the southern Levant began rebelling against Egyptian rule. The city of Per-Ramesses was built in the Delta after the Battle of Kadesh, ostensibly as a testament to Ramesses II's greatness, but also with the practical purpose of providing a staging point for potential military expeditions into the Levant and the Near East (Redford 1992, 185). Ramesses II led two expeditions in the eighth year of his reign into the southern Levant to suppress rebellions, one to the region of Galiee and another to Edom and Moab (Manley 1996, 93).

These expeditions were successful, with Ramesses bringing those regions back into the Egyptian fold, but the situation in the northern Levant was quite different. The Hittites eventually allowed Benteretire to return to Amurru, presumably after they realized the Egyptians were no longer a threat. Amurru would never return to Egyptian rule and Ramesses never attempted to reconquer it or Kadesh (Redford 1992, 185). Ramesses would use the Battle of Kadesh, through the Kadesh inscriptions, to create the impression that he was a great warrior, and although he likely acquitted himself well on the battlefield, other Egyptian pharaohs, notably Thutmose III, conquered far more territory and won many more battles.

This success convinced Ramesses II to push even further, and he expanded the power of the Egyptian Empire through continued conquests in 1272 B.C. and 1271 B.C., the eighth and ninth years of his reign. On these campaigns, he set his eyes upon conquests in the north, marching his army over the Dog River (Nahr el-Kelb) to Amurru, past Kadesh into Tunip, then on to Dapur.[7]

---

[7] Kitchen, Kenneth. 1996. *The Third Intermediate Period in Egypt (1100-650 BC)*. Aris & Phillips, Warminster. pp

It had been about 120 years since an Egyptian soldier had journeyed so far on a military campaign, dating back to the reign of Thutmose III. Statues and steles were erected at the sites of his many victories, including locations like Dapur, Beth Shean and Beirut.[8] It soon became apparent, however, that capturing territory between Amurru and Kadesh was easier than holding onto it. This contested borderland region between the Hittite and Egyptian empires was once again taken back by Hittite forces shortly after Ramesses II's campaigns, which led to yet another Egyptian campaign.

Ramesses marched his army to Dapur in 1270/1269 BCE, and the resulting battle came to be known as the Siege of Dapur. As with many of the battles fought by Ramesses II, the Siege of Dapur is recorded and illustrated on the wall of the Ramesseum in Thebes. The relief shows a heavily fortified city upon a rocky hill surrounded by fortified outer and inner walls. Ramesses II had taken even more of his many sons with him on this campaign, including Khamwese, Montu, Meriamon, Amenemuy, Seti and Setepnere. According to the images, there were chariots driven into battle, ladders used by soldiers to scale the walls, and archers firing arrows into the ranks of the opposing forces.[9] The location of the city of Dapur has been debated by academics, with one view identifying the location as Tabor in Canaan, while others interpret it as Syria to the north of Kadesh.[10] Wherever it was, the siege became a hotly contested area with both the Hittites and the Egyptians vying for control, but neither side was ever able to convincingly oust the other. It was an unstable possession for both sides of the conflict, making the only true losers the unfortunate people who lived there. They were pulled back and forth by the competing strengths of two vast empires.

26.

[8] Kitchen, Kenneth. 1996. *The Third Intermediate Period in Egypt (1100-650 BC)*. Aris & Phillips, Warminster. pp 223-224.

[9] Kitchen, Kenneth. 1998. *Ramesside Inscriptions*. Wiley-Blackwell. pp 56-83.

[10] Kitchen, Kenneth. 1996. *The Third Intermediate Period in Egypt (1100-650 BC)*. Aris & Phillips, Warminster. pp 26.

An ancient relief depicting the Siege of Dapur on a wall at Ramesseum

Aside from the edges of certain borders, the Egyptians and Hittites were able to tolerate each other's existence for the most part. But that nearly changed when a politically charged situation arose prior to 1258 BCE, Mursili III, a Hittite king, tried to depose his uncle, only to find himself deposed when his planned coup went awry. Fleeing for his life, he sought sanctuary in the court of Egypt, where Ramesses II chose to give him refuge. When the reigning king of the Hittite Empire, Hattusili III, demanded that Mursili III be surrendered, Ramesses II claimed to have no knowledge of the deposed king's whereabouts. The rising tensions surrounding that event almost led to all-out war between the two empires.[11] War was avoided on that occasion, and by now Ramesses II saw the benefits in negotiating some form of lasting peace.

Muwatalli may have been similar to Ramesses in many ways, but he did not share the Egyptian king's longevity. The Hittite king died two years after the Battle of Kadesh, and although the circumstances of his death are not related in texts, given that Muwatalli was the oldest son of his father and ruled for nearly 20 years, it is likely that he died of old age.

Mursili III (c. 1272-1267 BCE), the oldest son of Muwatalli, came to the Hittite throne. The new Hittite king faced a relatively stable situation in the northern Levant and a new threat to the southeast that threatened to destabilize the kingdom and his rule. When the Hittites toppled their old foe Mitanni, they apparently did not consider the long-term ramifications. Perhaps they were only thinking about how to expand into northern Mesopotamia and use that as a base for further operations in the Levant. The result was that once Mitanni was destroyed, the Assyrians stepped in to fill the vacuum, and as this was taking place the Hittites were still battling the rebellious Gasga people in northern Anatolia.

When the Assyrian King Shalmaneser I (ruled c. 1273-1244 BCE) led a major military campaign against the Kingdom of Urartu in what is today Armenia, Hattusili knew it was only a matter of time until the Assyrians turned to Hittite territory (Haywood 2005, 39). As a result, the Hittite king did what any effective ruler would do: he assessed the situation and decided that because Assyria posed more of a threat, he approached Egypt with a peace treaty and alliance. As a result, ironically, Ramesses II returned to Kadesh in 1258 BCE, this time end the ongoing fighting between the two empires once and for all.

The treaty text, from Ramesses II's 21st year of rule, begins with a bit of revisionist history about the relations between the two kingdoms before affirming oaths on the Egyptian sun-god and the Hittite storm-god: "Now I have established good brotherhood (and) good peace between us forever. In order to establish good peace (and) good brotherhood in [the relationship] of the land of Egypt with the Hatti land forever (I speak) thus: Behold, as for the relationship between the land of Egypt and the Hatti land, since eternity the god does not permit the making of hostility between them because of a treaty (valid) forever. Behold, Rea-Mashesha-Mai Amana, the great king, the king of the land of Egypt, in order to bring about the relationship that the Sun-god and the Storm-god have effected for the land of Egypt with the Hatti land finds himself in a relationship valid since eternity which [does not permit] the making of hostility between [them] until all and everlasting time." (Pritchard 1992, 202).

---

[11] Kitchen, Kenneth. 1982. *Pharaoh Triumphant: The Life and Times of Ramesses II, King of Egypt*. Mississauga, Benben Publications. pp 74.

The fact that the Battle of Kadesh was never mentioned is not surprising because it was probably a point of contention over who had actually won. The statements that both lands were friends "since eternity" is definitely interesting given that a massive battle in the area helped compel both sides to sign the treaty.

Other parts of the document are even more intriguing, and a later section that sets the limits of the empires does vaguely imply there once was a problem over the borders: "Rea-Mashesha-Mai Amana, the great king, the king of the land of Egypt, shall not trespass into the Hatti land to take anything therefrom in the future. And Hattusilis, the great king, the king of the Hatti land, shall not trespass into the land of Egypt to take anything therefrom in the future. Behold, the holy ordinance (valid) forever which the Sun-god and the Storm-god had brought about for the land of Egypt with the Hatti land (calls for) peace and brotherhood so as not to make hostility between them." (Pritchard 1992, 202).

The mere fact that these provisions had to be put in the treaty, and the use of the phrase "in the future," certainly eludes to the past conflicts between the two Great Powers without explicitly mentioning Kadesh. The text then continues to describe how the two powers had also become allies committed to each other's defense: "If an enemy from abroad comes against the Hatti land, and Hattusili, the great king, the king of the Hatti land, sends to me saying: "Come to me to help me against him," Rea-Mashesha-Mai Amana, the great king, the king of the land of Egypt, shall send his foot soldiers (and) his charioteers and they shall slay [his enemy and] take revenge upon him for the sake of the Hatti land…If an enemy from abroad comes against the land of Egypt and Rea-Mashesha-Mai Amana, the king of the land of Egypt, your brother, sends to Hattusilis, the king of the Hatti land, his brother, saying: 'Come here to help me against him' – lo! Hattusilis, the king of the Hatti land, shall send his foot soldiers (and) his charioteers and shall slay my enemies." (Pritchard 1992, 202).

The treaty also relates how each signatory was obligated to return fugitives who fled to the other side (Pritchard 1992, 203). With that, the relations were cemented with a diplomatic marriage. Ramesses II enjoyed collecting brides, and this occasion gave him a chance to take a Hittite princess. A stela from the Abu Simbel Temple in Nubia relates how Hattusili sent "Mahorneferure, daughter of the chief of Kheta" to marry the Egyptian king (Breasted 2001, 182). The princess was likely brought to Egypt with a large entourage, including possibly Hattusili himself, where they were greeted with a great feast (Breasted 2001, 183). Ramesses, of course, never thought of sending one of his daughters to Hattusili, but, by then, the two old foes had put the Battle of Kadesh behind them and looked forward to a new future.

Part of a written tablet that contained the terms of the peace treaty

Although the frontiers of the empires were not mapped out specifically in the treaty, they were inferred by references to particular towns, cities and regions, such as Canaan and coastal towns of Phonecia, which were named as being under Egyptian control. After the treaty, the northern-most town belonging to Egypt, and the one holding the furthest placed garrison of Egyptian forces, became Sumur, a harbor settlement located to the north of Byblos.[12]

The treaty ensured the safety and security of Egypt's northern borders, a safety that was to last uncontested until after the death of Ramesses II. The treaty also ended the military expansionist

[12] Grimal, Nicolas. 1994. *A History of Ancient Egypt.* Wiley, USA. pp 256.

campaigns of Ramesses II into Hittite territory. He had succeeded in expanding his borders, but more importantly the treaty secured those borders without the need for ongoing battle to hold contested ground. In the years of peace that followed, Ramesses II was able to devote his energies to another legacy, the other main activity apart from warfare that would ensure his historic longevity: the building of monuments.

The long reign of Ramesses the Great created problems with royal succession. He outlived most of his scores of children, which meant that even once a successor was chosen, the dynasty was close to an end. The advanced age of Ramesses II may also point toward poor policy decisions made late in his kingship, which was a time when decisive leaders were needed to deal with threats from abroad.

Ramesses II was eventually succeeded by one of his sons, Merenptah (ca. 1224-1204 BCE). By all accounts Merenptah was an able king, but most of his rule was consumed with fighting foreign invaders. Incursions by the Libyans from the west became common during Ramesses II's rule, although they were for the most part little more than a nuisance at that time. During the rule of Merenptah, the threat became existential when the Libyans united with five tribes of the so-called Sea Peoples. The war against the Sea Peoples and Libyans took place in Merenptah's fifth year and was commemorated in hieroglyphs on a stela in the Karnak Temple. Part of the inscription reads, "The wretched, fallen chief of Libya, Meryey, son of Ded, has fallen upon the country of Tehenu with his bowmen . . . Sherden, Shekelesh, Ekwesh, Luka, Teresh, taking the best of every warrior and every man of war of his country. He has brought his wife and his children . . . leaders of the camp, and he has reached the western boundary in the fields of Perire. . . Lo, the bowman of his majesty spent six hours of destruction among them; they were delivered to the sword upon . . . of the country. Lo, as they fought . . .; the wretched chief of Libya halted, his heart fearing; withdrew (again), stopped, knelt, . . . [leaving] sandals, his bow, and his quiver in haste behind [him], and every [thing] that was with him. [. . .] his limbs, great terror coursed in his members. Lo, [they] slew . . . of his possessions, his [equipment], his silver, his gold, his arrows, all his works, which he had brought from his land, consisting of oxen, goats, and asses [and all were carried away] to the palace, to bring the in, together with the captives." (Breasted 2001, 3:243-6).

According to the stela, over 6,000 Libyans and 1,000 Sea Peoples were listed as casualties of the war, which indicates that it was no mere skirmish (Breasted 2001, 3:248-9). Merenptah saved Egypt from the fate of annihilation, which the Sea Peoples subsequently meted out to the Hittites, but the trajectory of the New Kingdom was clearly on a downward trend.

The end of the Nineteenth Dynasty brought forth turmoil over succession issues, but once the smoke cleared, the Twentieth Dynasty was established. Although not directly related to the kings of the Nineteenth Dynasty, the Twentieth Dynasty is also considered part of the Ramesside

Period, largely due to the fact that many of its kings were named Ramesses. Most of the kings of the Twentieth Dynasty did little of importance, with the exception of Ramesses III (1184-1152 BCE). Ramesses III was the son and successor of Sethnakht (1186-1184 BCE), who he credited with reestablishing order in Egypt, in numerous texts, or *maat* (Kuhrt 2010, 1:204).

Ramesses III, like his more famous namesake, was a prolific builder in his own right. He built the great temple complex near the modern village of Medinet Habu, which functioned primarily as his mortuary complex (Haeny 1997, 107). Ramesses III even honored his predecessor at Medinet Habu by constructing a chapel dedicated to the cult of the divine Ramesses II (Haeny 1997, 109). Besides its size, Medinet Habu stands apart from most other Egyptian temples because it had an outer wall and gates (Haney 1997, 121). Although other New Kingdom temples were built with walls, they were meant to divide sections of the temple available to the public and those that only priests could enter. The temple complex at Medinet Habu doubled as a fortress, which was a sign of the extremely unstable times.

Steve F-E Cameron's pictures of Medinet Habu

A relief from the Karnak Temple depicting Ramesses III

The walls of the Medinet Habu Temple and several extant papyri describe the precarious situation in which Ramesses III found himself. Like Merenptah, Ramesses III had to contend with a major assault from the Sea Peoples and two major wars with the Libyans. Unlike the assault during the reign of Merenptah, which came from the Libyan Desert, the attack in Ramesses III's eighth year came from the Levant.

The texts lists five different Sea Peoples tribes in the war, but some are different than those that participated in the attack on Merenptah. Ramesses III was ultimately successful, as related in the Medinet Habu inscriptions. "The countries . . . the [Northerners] in their isles were disturbed, taken away in the fray . . .at one time. Not one stood before their hands, from Kheta, Kode, Carchemish, Arvad, Alasa, they were wasted. [The]y [set up] a camp in one place in Amor. They desolated his people and his land like that which is not. They came with fire prepared before them, forward to Egypt. Their main support was Peleset, Thekel, Shekelesh, Denyen, and Weshesh, (these) lands were united, and they laid their hands upon the land as far as the Circle of the Earth. Their hearts confident, full of their plans. . . I equipped my frontier in   Zahi, prepared before them. The chiefs, the captains of infantry, the nobles, I caused to equip the harbor-mouths, like a strong wall, with warships, galleys, and barges, [. . .]. They were manned [completely] from bow to stern with valiant warriors bearing their arms, soldiers of all the choicest of Egypt, being like lions roaring upon the mountain-tops. . . Those who reached my boundary, their seed is not; their heart and their soul are finished forever and ever. As for those who had assembled before them on the sea, the full flame was in their front, before the harbor-mouths, and a wall of metal upon the shore surrounded them. They were dragged, overturned, and laid low upon the beach; slain and made heaps from stern to bow of their galleys, while all their things were cast upon the water." (Breasted 2001, 4:37-39)

The attempted Sea Peoples invasion was not the end of Ramesses III's troubles. He also had to contend with two major wars against the Libyans. Interactions with the Libyans had been a normal part of life for the Egyptians since the Old Kingdom. Unlike the Nubians, the Libyans had little material wealth for the Egyptians to exploit, so apart from an occasional putative raid, they left the nomadic tribes alone for the most part. As the Libyan population increased, though, the desert tribes began to move east into the Nile Delta.

The Libyan alliance with the Sea Peoples during Merenptah's reign represented something new – the Libyans had become organized into a more cohesive political unit. A chieftain named Themer led the Chemah/Temeh Libyan tribe against Ramesses III in a fairly well-organized attack. An inscription from Medinet Habu reads, "The land of Temeh is spread out, they flee. The Meshwesh are hung up in their land, their plant are uprooted, there is not for them a survivor. All their limbs tremble for the terror, which protects against them. They say: "Behold, we are [subject] to Egypt, its lord has destroyed our soul, forever and ever . . . The fire has penetrated us, our seed is not. As for Ded, Meshken, Meryey and Wermer, Themer, and every hostile chief who crossed the border of Egypt from Libya, he hath set fire from front to rear." (Breasted 2001, 4:23-24).

Although Ramesses III was successful, it did not deter the Libyans from reorganizing and attacking Egypt again. The Second Libyan War began after a chieftain named Keper led the Libyan tribe known as the Meshwesh against another Libyan tribe known as the Chenu/Tjehnu (Wainwright 1962, 89). The result was an imbalance in the power structure that Ramesses III had to rectify. "[The foe] had allied themselves against Egypt, the god permitting that they should [lead on to mount their horses], (but) mighty was the valor of him who is the sole lord, and his talons [made ready] like a [trap] at their arrival, when they came with restless limbs to lay themselves like mice under his arms, the king, Ramesses III. As for the (chief of) Meshwesh, since he appeared, he went to one place, his land with him, and invaded the Tehenu, who were made ashes, spoiled and desolated were their cities, their seed was not. They [disregarded] the beauty of this god who slays the invader of Egypt, saying… 'We will settle in Egypt.'" (Breasted 2001, 4:52).

Ramesses III's turbulent reign ended most inauspiciously with his assassination, which was actually recorded on two papyrus scrolls (Kuhrt 2010, 1:187). His death was followed by a succession of several weak rulers, ushering in the end of the New Kingdom and pharaonic Egypt's greatest period.

Online Resources

<u>Other books about ancient history by Charles River Editors</u>

Further Reading

Breasted, James Henry, ed. and trans. 2001. *Ancient Records of Egypt.* Vol. 4, *The Nineteenth Dynasty.* Champaign, Illinois: University of Illinois Press.

Bryce, Trevor B. 2007. *The Kingdom of the Hittites.* New ed. Oxford: Oxford University Press.

Cochavi-Rainey, Zipora, trans and ed. 1999. *Royal Gifts in the Late Bronze Age Fourteenth to Thirteenth Centuries B.C.E.: Selected Texts Recording Gifts to Royal Personages.* Jerusalem: Ben-Gurion University of the Negev Press.

Dijk, Jacobus van. 2000. "The Amarna Period and the Later New Kingdom." In *The Oxford History of Ancient Egypt*, edited by Ian Shaw, 272-313. Oxford: Oxford University Press.

Faulkner, Richard O. 1999. *A Concise Dictionary of Middle Egyptian.* Oxford: Griffith Institute.

Goedicke, Hans. 1984. "The Canaanite Illness." *Studien zur altägyptische Kultur* 11: 91-105.

Kuhrt, Amélie. 2010. *The Ancient Near East: c. 3000-330 BC.* 2 vols. London: Routledge.

Lesko, Leonard. *A Dictionary of Late Egyptian.* 2 Vols. Fall River, Massachusetts: Fall River Modern Printing Company, 2002.

Lichtheim, Miriam, ed. 1976. *Ancient Egyptian Literature: A Book of Reading.* Vol. 2, *The New Kingdom.* Los Angeles: University of California Press.

Macqueen, J.G. 2003. *The Hittites and Their Contemporaries in Asia Minor.* London: Thames and Hudson.

Mieroop, Marc van de. 2007. *A History of the Ancient Near East: ca. 3000-323 BC*. 2nd ed. London: Blackwell.

Moran, William L., ed. and trans. 1992. *The Amarna Letters*. Baltimore: John Hopkins University Press.

Murnane, William J. trans. 1995. *Texts from the Amarna Period in Egypt*. Atlanta: Scholars Press.

Pritchard, James B., ed. 1992. *Ancient Near Eastern Texts Relating to the Old Testament*. 3rd ed. Princeton, New Jersey: Princeton University Press.

Redford, Donald B. 1986. *Pharaonic King-Lists, Annals and Day-Books: A Contribution to the Study of the Egyptian Sense of History*. Mississauga, Canada: Benben Publications.

———. 1992. *Egypt, Canaan, and Israel in Ancient Times*. Princeton, New Jersey: Princeton University Press.

Sandars, Nancy. 1987. *The Sea Peoples: Warriors of the Ancient Mediterranean, 1250-1150 BC*. Rev. ed. London: Thames and Hudson.

Schulman, Alan R. 1979. "Diplomatic Marriage in the Egyptian New Kingdom." *Journal of Near Eastern Studies* 38: 177-193.

———. 1978. "Ankhesenamun, Nofretity, and the Amka Affair." *Journal of the American Research Center in Egypt* 15: 43-48.

Shaw, Ian and Paul Nicholson. 1995. *The Dictionary of Ancient Egypt*. New York: Harry N. Abrams.

Spalinger, Anthony. 2005. *War in Ancient Egypt*. London: Blackwell.